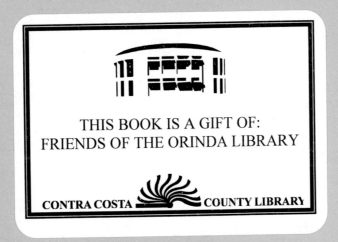

I Love to Paint!

Jennifer Lipsey

LARK BOOKS

A Division of Sterling Publishing Co., Inc.
New York

My Very Favorite Art Book

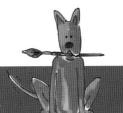

This book is dedicated
to my niece Sidney,
the expert texture
treasure hunter.

Editor
JOE RHATIGAN

Creative Director
CELIA NARANJO

Associate Art Director
SHANNON YOKELEY

Editorial Assistance
DELORES GOSNELL

Library of Congress Cataloging-in-Publication Data

Lipsey, Jennifer.
  My very favorite art book : I love to paint / Jennifer Lipsey.
     p. cm.
  Includes bibliographical references and index.
  ISBN 1-57990-630-3 (hardcover)
  1. Painting—Technique. 2. Handicraft. I. Title: I love to paint. II. Title.
  ND1473.L57 2005
  751.4—dc22

                                   2005013200

10 9 8 7 6 5 4 3 2

Published by Lark Books, A Division of
Sterling Publishing Co., Inc.
387 Park Avenue South, New York, N.Y. 10016

© 2005, Jennifer Lipsey

Distributed in Canada by Sterling Publishing,
c/o Canadian Manda Group, 165 Dufferin Street
Toronto, Ontario, Canada M6K 3H6

Distributed in the United Kingdom by GMC Distribution Services,
Castle Place, 166 High Street, Lewes, East Sussex, England BN7 1XU

Distributed in Australia by Capricorn Link (Australia) Pty Ltd.
P.O. Box 704, Windsor, NSW 2756 Australia

The written instructions, photographs, designs, patterns, and projects in this volume are intended for the personal use of the reader and may be reproduced for that purpose only. Any other use, especially commercial use, is forbidden under law without written permission of the copyright holder.

Every effort has been made to ensure that all the information in this book is accurate. However, due to differing conditions, tools, and individual skills, the publisher cannot be responsible for any injuries, losses, and other damages that may result from the use of the information in this book.

If you have questions or comments about this book, please contact:
Lark Books
67 Broadway
Asheville, NC 28801
(828) 253-0467

Manufactured in China

ISBN 13: 978-1-57990-630-6
ISBN 10: 1-57990-630-3

For information about custom editions, special sales, premium and corporate purchases, please contact Sterling Special Sales Department at 800-805-5489 or specialsales@sterlingpub.com.

CONTENTS

Paint is Great!

Painting is fun, and anyone can do it!

All you really need to get started is paint and something to paint on.

A paintbrush is handy, too, if you don't always want to paint with your fingers.

Your paintings can look like something real...

But they don't have to.

Both are awesome!

This book will show you lots of cool ways to paint. You will see how to paint with sponges, toothpicks, rollers, and even straws! There are loads of projects and examples so you will never run out of ideas.

This is a roller. It's also called a brayer.

Painting goes all the way back to caveman (and woman) times. Even then, cave dwellers had to gather their supplies before they started painting, and so will you.

Supplies

Paint Brushes

come in many shapes and sizes.

Small brushes are good for painting small shapes and details.

Take good care of your brushes by washing them out with warm water when you're done.

Large, flat brushes are good for big shapes and spaces. Practice different brush strokes with your paintbrushes.

Paint

In this book, we will work with lots of different art supplies.

These are the three main paints we will be working with:

Paint

Watercolors

Crayons

Tempera paints and poster paints are the same thing.

They come in bottles or jars.

The paint is ready to use as soon as you open it. You can use acrylic paints, too.

Watercolor paints usually come in a case like this one.

You have to wet this paint first to make it work.

Yes, you can paint with crayons!

Keep your broken crayons handy. You'll see why.

a Palette

This is the thing that holds your paint. It's easier to mix colors if you use one.

A palette doesn't have to be fancy.

It can be something you can use over and over again, such as a dinner plate or an old cookie sheet.

Or, it can be something you throw out when you're done, such as a foam plate.

Here's how to make your own palette.

1. Staple 10 pieces of waxed paper to a piece of cardboard.

2. The waxed paper is your palette. Simply rip off the top sheet when you're done painting. The next sheet is clean!

Paper

You can paint on most any kind of paper.

Some projects in this book call for thin paper, while others work better on thick paper.

Here are ideas for thin and thick papers you might find for free:

newspaper
junk mail
wrapping paper

computer paper

coffee
filters

Thin

cereal boxes   manila
folders
construction
paper   old greeting
cards
cardboard

Thick

Set Up

1. Put on some old clothes or an apron.
2. Lay out some newspaper, an old sheet, or a shower curtain to protect the table or floor you are going to be working on.
3. Get out your supplies and this book. Have fun!

Clean Up

1. Lay your paintings someplace safe to dry.
2. Throw out the used water. Wash your brushes and tools.
3. Put everything away.
4. Throw out the newspaper or fold up the sheet.

HINT: Adults will let you paint more often if you keep your art things clean and neat. Guaranteed!

Make an Art Kit

Use a cardboard box or a plastic bin to hold all of your art supplies. This will be your Art Kit.

With an Art Kit, you will always know where your supplies are, and it makes set up and clean up much easier.

Here are supplies to include in your Art Kit:

- Paint
- Pencils
- Eraser
- Markers
- Crayons
- Brushes
- Palette
- Paper
- Glue
- Water container
- Rollers and cans
- Sponges
- Old toothbrush
- Scissors
- Paper towels
- Cardboard tubes
- Newspaper

Color

The only colors you really need are red, yellow, blue, black, and white. With some color math you can mix any color you want.

Here's how:

 Red + Blue = Purple

 Yellow + Red = Orange

 Blue + Yellow = Green

What happens when you add white or black to a color?

Mix SKIN Colors

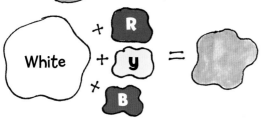 White + R + y + B =

Start with white. Add a little of the three primary colors until you get the skin color you want.

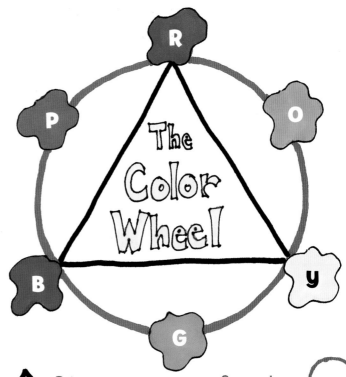

The Color Wheel

△ Primary Colors

These make other colors:
Red
Yellow
Blue

○ Secondary Colors

These are made from primary colors:
Purple
Orange
Green

Let's Paint!

Finger-paint Fun!

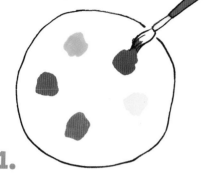

1. Put small puddles of paint on your palette.

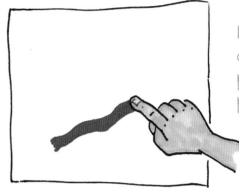

If you want, draw a picture in pencil first.

2. Now touch your finger to a paint puddle. Use your finger like a paintbrush.

Don't forget to wipe your finger on a paper towel when you want to change colors.

Fill up the whole page.

3. Try using different fingers. What happens if you use two or three fingers at once?

Supplies
* Tempera paint
* Palette
* Paper
* Paper towels
* Your fingers!

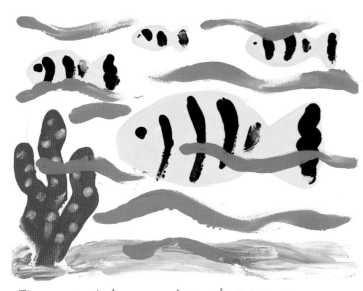

Finger-paint an underwater scene.

Why not try a prehistoric scene?

Use fingerprints for the sun and the coconuts.

Wild Watercolors!

1.
Lightly draw a shape with your pencil.

2.

Carefully paint the whole shape with clear water.

3.

Use the other brush to put watercolor on the wet shape.

The paint will stay inside the shape!

Paint until the shape is filled with color.

Supplies
* Pencil
* Thick paper
* 2 paintbrushes
* Water cup
* Watercolor paint

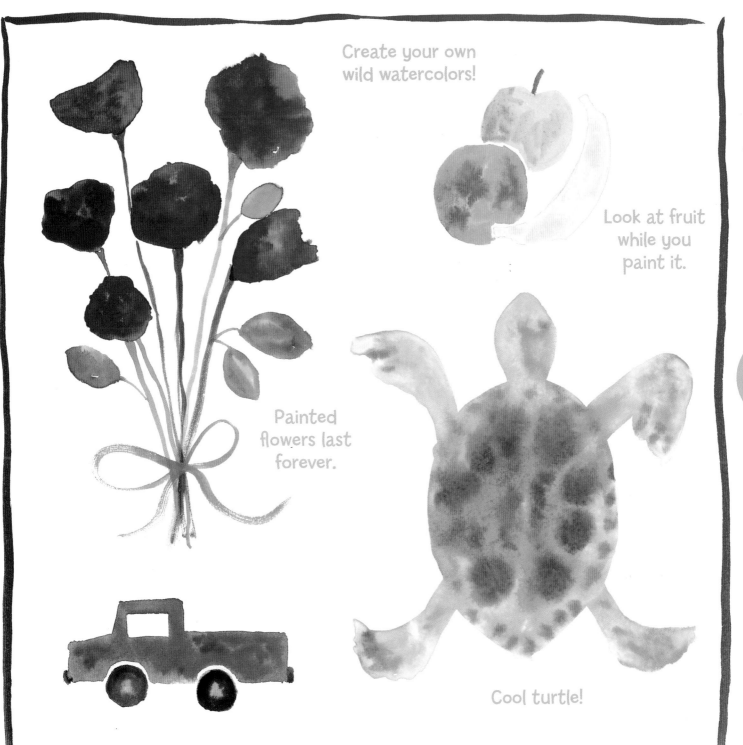

Create your own
wild watercolors!

Look at fruit
while you
paint it.

Painted
flowers last
forever.

Cool turtle!

Blob & Blot

1. Fold a piece of paper in half.

2. Unfold the paper, and put a few drops of paint near the middle.

3. Fold the paper in half again. Press and rub all over the paper.

4. Open the paper again. If you like what you see, let it dry.

Or, you can add more paint and fold it again. Let it dry.

Now look closely at your paint blot. Do you see something in it?

Use markers to add details.

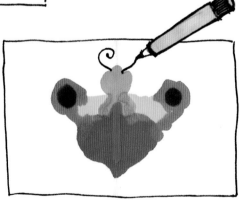

5.

Supplies
* Paper
* Tempera paint
* Palette
* Paintbrush
* Water cup
* Markers

Use markers to add details to your paint blot. What do you see in your paint blots?

A butterfly?

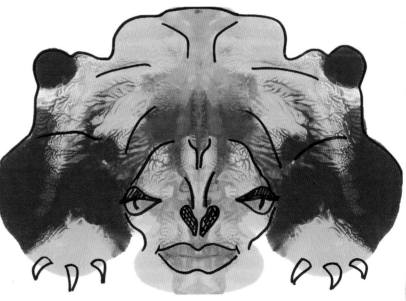

A monster?

Tape Painting

1.

Make a picture with pieces of masking tape.

2.

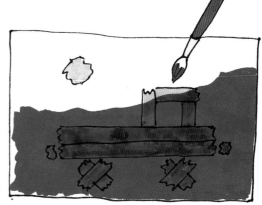

Paint over your tape picture. Let your colors mix together if you want.

3.

After the painting dries, peel off the tape. Awesome!

Try this!
Make a tape picture on top of a finished painting. Paint it again, and remove the tape. Wow!

Supplies
* Paper
* Masking tape
* Watercolor paint
* Paintbrush
* Water cup

Try a flower!

Scratch Magic!

1. Draw a picture with a pencil very lightly.

2. Firmly scratch over the pencil lines with a pushpin or other tool. Erase the pencil lines.

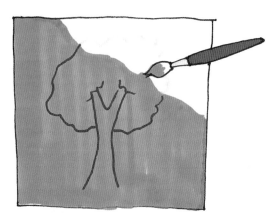

3. Paint over your whole picture. Your drawing appears like magic!

Supplies
* Thick paper
* Pencil
* Pushpin, nail, or large paperclip
* Eraser
* Watercolor paint
* Paintbrush
* Water cup

18

Try different colors!

You can use a tissue to blot parts you want to make lighter.

Watch out for that shark!

Rock & Roll

1.

Paint your roller.

Roll on moist paper towels to clean the roller.

2.

Roll it onto the paper.

3.

See what happens when you paint a shape on the roller.

Cool!

Supplies
* Roller
* Tempera paint
* Palette
* Paintbrush
* Water cup
* Paper

Roll a giant.

Use your roller to create the body. Paint small trees or houses to show how big he (or she!) is.

Use a sponge for the giant's hair and for the treetops.

Roller designs also make a nice background for drawings.

Roll a cool design by overlapping different colors.

Sponge Blob!

Sponges come in many sizes, shapes, and colors. Have a parent cut a big sponge into small, easy-to-hold pieces.

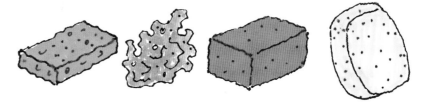

1.

Brush or squirt colors you want to use onto your palette.

2.

Dip the sponge in some paint. See what happens when you twist, blot, and sweep the sponge on the paper.

> **Clean your sponges by dipping them in water and squeezing all the paint out.**

Try this!

Wet your paper with water and a clean sponge. Then, sponge paint on the wet paper. So cool!

or

Use scissors to cut shapes from a thin sponge. Use them like stamps.

Supplies
* Sponges
* Scissors
* Tempera paint
* Palette
* Paintbrush
* Water cup
* Paper

SPONGE

You can buy sponges that are already cut into shapes.

Cut out shapes to make a picture.

Use the corners, edges, and sides of the sponge.

Try twists, dots, and lines on wet paper.

Dot to Dot

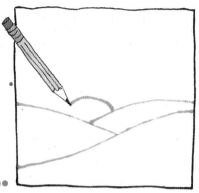

1. Lightly draw a simple picture with a pencil.

Gently press the eraser on your paint pad.

2.

3. Fill up one section of your picture with dots.

> **When you're ready to change colors, clean the eraser by blotting it on a moist paper towel.**

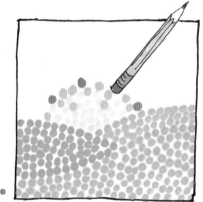

4.

Fill in other sections of your picture with dots.

Make a Paint Pad

1. Fold a wet paper towel to fit on top of a plate.

2. Brush paint on the paper towel.

Make a paint pad for each color you use.

Supplies
* Paper
* Pencil with a new eraser
* Paper towels
* Water
* Plate
* Tempera paint

24

Trace something square or round.

Make dot frames for your favorite paintings.

Mix your colors!

How about a dotted sunrise?

Try some flowers.

Use a brush to paint the stems.

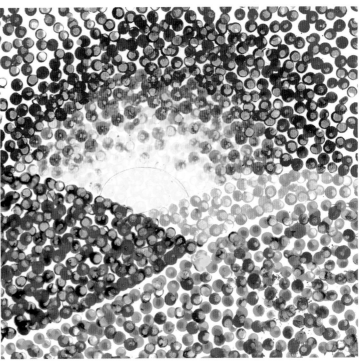

Finger Printing

Did you know you can paint lots of different shapes with your fingers? Check it out!

 Thumb

 Index finger

Middle finger

Ring finger

 Side of the pinky

Pinky   Ring   Middle   Index   Thumb

Practice these prints by pressing the underside of your fingertips onto the paint pad. Then press your finger onto the paper.

Soft ring finger: Press gently to make a small print.

Hard ring finger: Press harder to make a big print.

Try this!

Index

Thumb

Thumb sideways

1.

Pinky side

Pinky side

2.

Pinky side

Ring soft

Ring hard

3.

Supplies

* Paint pads (see page 24)
* Tempera paint
* Paper
* Your fingers

Can you figure out which fingers were used to make these pictures?

Where's my suntan lotion?

Touchdown!

Wet Wax!

1. Draw a picture with your pencil.

2. Color it in with crayons. Press down hard, and leave a little white paper showing.

3. Paint the whole picture with black paint. Looks awesome, doesn't it?

Try This!

1. Use a black crayon to draw your picture. Don't forget to press down hard.

2. Color your picture in with crayons. Leave some white showing. Then, paint it with bright watercolors.

Supplies
* Pencil
* Paper
* Crayons
* Watercolor paints
* Paintbrush
* Water cup

Look in the mirror
and try drawing a
self-portrait.

How about a
toucan in the
jungle?

Super Stencil!

1.

Fold your piece of paper in half. Draw half of a shape on it.

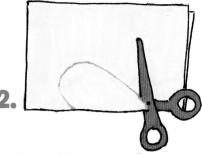

2.

Keep the paper folded and cut out the shape. Open up the two pieces.

3.

Dip your paintbrush in some paint. Brush most of the paint onto a paper towel.

4.

Hold the stencil on a new piece of paper. Start on the stencil and brush toward the middle.

5.

Try using the other piece you cut out in step 2. Paint away from the shape.

Supplies

* Thick paper
* Pencil
* Scissors
* Tempera paint
* Palette
* Flat paintbrush
* Water cup
* Paper towels

Here you can see both pieces.

Try overlapping shapes and colors.

Make a mountain stencil.

Soggy Art!

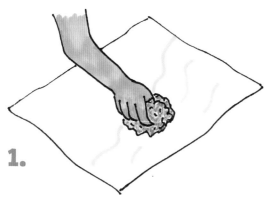

1. Use a wet sponge to moisten the paper all over.

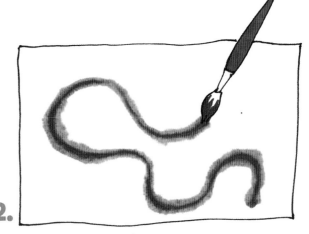

2. Paint on the wet paper. Watch the colors spread out and blend together.

Don't forget to wash your paintbrush before you change colors.

Try this!

1. Wet the paper. Paint a sky and leave the ground white.

2. While the paper is still wet, paint lines where you want trees.

3. Paint tall squiggly triangle shapes on the lines.

Supplies
* Thick paper
* Wet sponge
* Tempera paint
* Palette
* Paintbrush
* Water cup

Paint a squiggly line all over your wet paper. Fill in the leftover spaces with a different color.

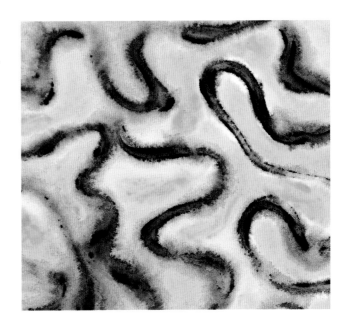

Try using lots of different colors on the wet paper.

Straw Painting

1.

Put a small puddle of watercolor or watered down tempera paint on your paper.

2.

Aim the straw where you want the paint to move and BLOW!

Try blowing with two straws at the same time.

Try this!

1.

Paint a sunset with black land. Let it dry.

A sunset silhouette!

2.

Blow black trees up from the land.

Supplies
* Paper
* Paintbrush
* Watercolor paint or watered-down tempera paint
* Water cup
* Straws

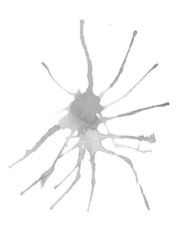

Try mixing up
your colors.

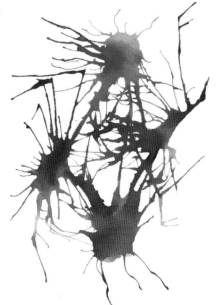

On a Roll!

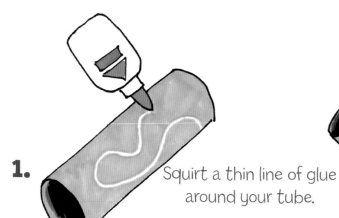

1. Squirt a thin line of glue around your tube.

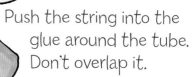

2. Push the string into the glue around the tube. Don't overlap it.

Make sure there aren't any loose spots where the string isn't glued. Let it dry.

3. When the glue is dry, paint the string. Now roll it across the paper to see the string design.

Try this!

Cut out small cardboard or foam shapes and glue them to a tube.

Paint the shapes and roll the tube to see the pattern. Wow!

Supplies
* Cardboard tubes
* Glue
* String
* Tempera paint
* Paintbrush
* Palette
* Water cup
* Paper
* Cardboard
* Scissors

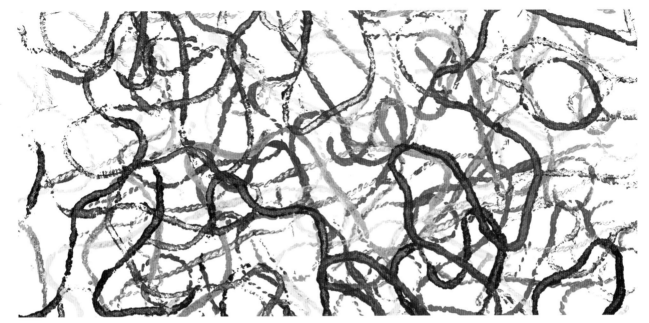

Try different colors on the same string.

Make different color prints from the same tube.

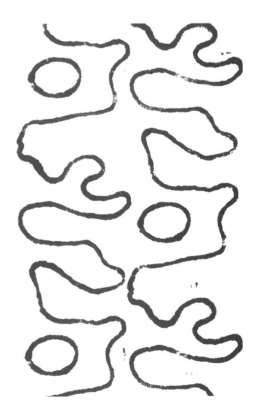

All Cracked Up!

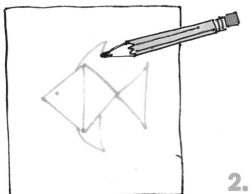

1. Draw a picture with a pencil.

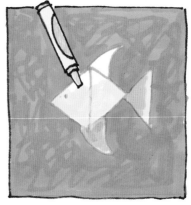

2. Color it in with crayons. Use bright colors and press hard. Color in all the white parts.

3. Crumple up your picture! Smooth it out and crumple it again.

4. Smooth out the paper. Paint over it with a dark color.

5. Gently rinse the paint off. Stop when there's only paint left in the cracks. Let it dry.

Supplies
* Pencil
* Paper
* Crayons
* Tempera paint
* Paintbrush
* Palette
* Water cup
* Sink

Draw a flamingo!

If you need to flatten your painting more, put it between two sheets of paper and have a parent iron it on low heat.

Scratch It!

1. Color your paper all over with bright colors. Press hard and cover all the white parts of your paper.

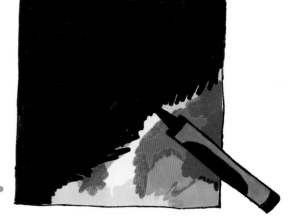

2. Color your paper over with the black crayon. Press hard and cover all the colors.

3.

Use the nail, toothpick, or even your fingernail to scratch your picture.

Awesome!

Supplies

* Crayons
* Paper
* Nail, toothpick, paperclip, or something you can scratch with

How about a dragon?

You can "erase" a mistake by coloring over it with a black crayon.

Play & Spray!

How to spray paint:

1. Dip the toothbrush in a small paint puddle.

2. Hold the brush down over the paper.

Pull the bristles toward you with your finger.

The paint will spray away from you.

Re-dip when you start to run out of spray.

Clean the toothbrush between colors by swishing it in water. Dry it on a paper towel.

Now, for even more FUN!

1. Find flat things in and around your home. You can also cut out paper shapes. Place them on your paper.

2. Spray paint on top of the objects. Remove the objects after the paint dries. Cool!

Supplies
* Tempera paint
* Palette
* Old toothbrush
* Water cup
* Paper
* Flat objects

Make your initials with string.

Paint the paper first, and after it's dry, spray something over it.

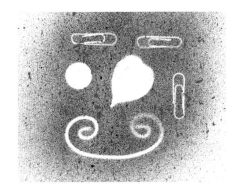

Try different designs.

· Make a snowman!

Texture Treasures

Touch different things you see around you. The bottom of your shoe, a wall, screens, wood—these things feel different because they have different surface textures.

Crayon rubbings are pictures of each texture.

1. Find a texture and hold the paper on top of it. Rub the side of an unwrapped crayon across the paper.

2. Find more textures, and make more rubbings on the same paper.

Try this!

See what happens when you paint with watercolors on top of your textured pictures.

It's cool!

Supplies
* Crayons
* Thin paper
* Textured objects
* Watercolor paint
* Paintbrush
* Water cup

Try lots of colors on one texture.

Paint it!

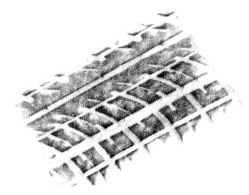

Can you guess what this is?

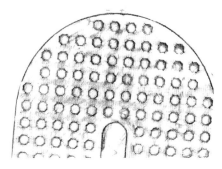

Textures are everywhere!

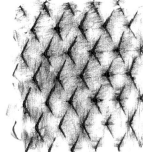

Try different colors. Let the textures overlap.

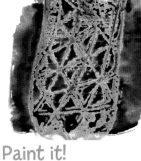

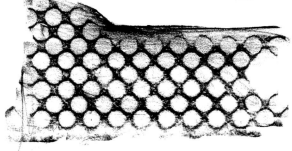

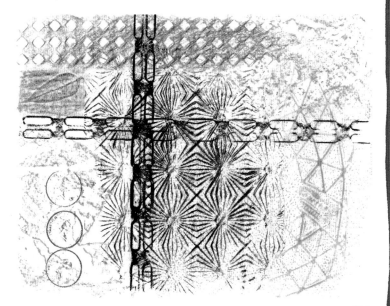

String's the Thing!

1. Cut a piece of string or yarn about as long as your arm. Drop one end into a can of paint.

> Use a different piece of string for each color.

2. Slowly pull the string out, and remove extra paint by squeezing it between a brush and the inside of the can.

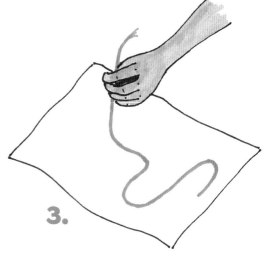

3. Put the wet string on the paper. Drag it up, down, and all around. Use a new string and can for each color.

Try this!

1. Fold a piece of paper.

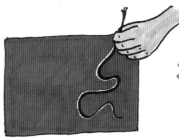

2. Unfold it and place a painted string on one side. Hold onto one end of the string.

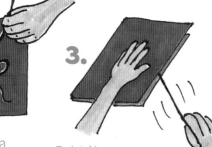

3. Fold the paper, and hold it closed while you wiggle the string out. Open the paper. Wow!

Supplies
* String or yarn
* Scissors
* Tempera paint
* Cans
* Paintbrush
* Paper

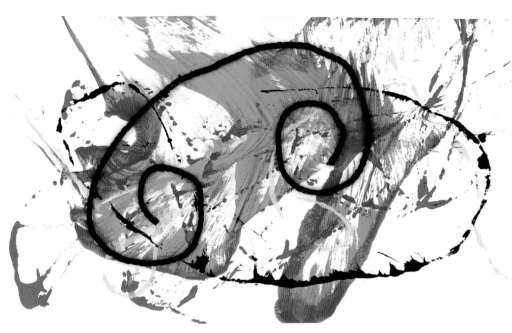

You can even glue your dried, painted string to the painting.

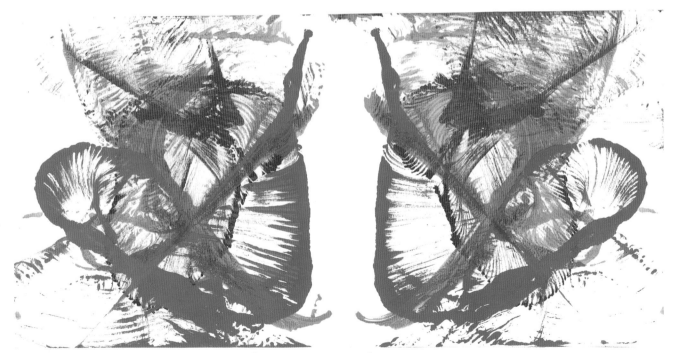

This design was done with a folded piece of paper.

Acknowledgements

I would like to thank my students at Veritas who have been such an inspiration and have kid-tested nearly all the projects in this book. Thank you to my parents and family, friends, colleagues, and Lark staff who have been so supportive and encouraging over the past year. Special thanks to my husband, Martin, for all the love, good coffee, late nights, and lost weekends. Lastly, heartfelt thanks to the great Artist for passing along such wonderful things as the need and the means to create.

Index